WIDE F
SCIENCE S   3

Michael Holt and
Alan Ward

Oliver & Boyd

Illustrated by Moira Chesmur

Oliver & Boyd
Robert Stevenson House
1–3 Baxter's Place
Leith Walk
Edinburgh EH1 3BB
A Division of Longman Group Ltd

ISBN 0 05 003292 5

First published 1983

Set in Monophoto Plantin 12/18pt
Printed in Hong Kong
by Sheck Wah Tong Printing Press Ltd

Preface

This series is an attempt to introduce junior school children to important ideas and experiences in science through the medium of stories. It is not in any way a science course, but we hope that it may be helpful in expanding the range and content of children's reading and introducing them to the world of science. The stories have all been chosen to relate to the kind of ideas the intended young reader finds comprehensible and interesting.

The four books of the series are written for children of reading ages 7+ to 11+. Book One is broadly suitable for children of reading age 7+ to 8+, Book Two for 8+ to 9+, Book Three for 9+ to 10+ and Book Four for 10+ to 11+.

Contents

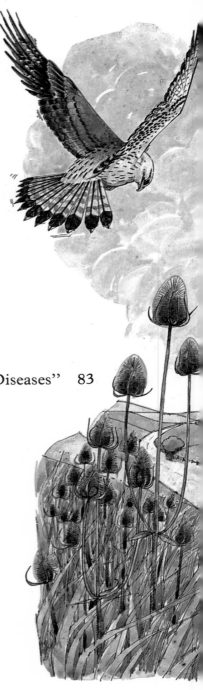

The Return of the Fish-Hawk

A hunting osprey is a grand sight. Spying its prey
from high above a lake, the osprey drops down with
almost closed wings, making a great splash as it
enters the water. Then it rises again, with a fish
grasped like a limp torpedo in its sickle-shaped
claws.

An osprey is a *predator* — that is, it catches its
food alive. Blackbirds and kingfishers are predators,
too. The blackbird tugs worms from their holes in
the lawn, and the beautiful kingfisher plunges into
running water after small fish. Many predators,
especially crows, will also eat dead meat or *carrion*
as it is called.

Other predatory birds are owls, hawks, falcons
and eagles. These all have sharp, hooked beaks
and claws, needed for tearing the flesh of animals
like mice, voles and rabbits — and even lizards,
frogs and fish.

Owls hunt mostly by night, using their
extra-sensitive hearing rather than their excellent
eyesight. Birds of prey such as hawks and falcons,
however, do their hunting by day; they too have
good eyesight. Some birds of prey are fairly
common. You may have seen a falcon called the
kestrel, hovering with its tail feathers spread in a
fan over the grass verge of a motorway, searching
for small animals. But many other British birds of
prey such as the golden eagle, the peregrine falcon
and the red kite (which breeds only in Wales) are
very rare.

Golden eagle

Peregrine
falcon

Carrion
crow

Blackbird

Tawny
owl

Red kite

Kingfisher

One of the rarest and most impressive of all is the fish-eating osprey, also called the fish-hawk. From a distance, an osprey looks like a big black and white bird. Close to, its head, neck and under parts are white. The upper parts are very dark brown.

It is a very big bird, and its powerful wings have a span of over one and a half metres. With these wings and its short strong tail, an osprey can hover like a helicopter or soar like a glider. Its favourite food is pike and trout, and it spends most of its time flying over dense forests and lakes in the wild places of the world. It is found mainly in America, Australia and in the northern parts of Europe, but there are a few ospreys in Britain. They live mostly in the Scottish mountains and hunt for fish in the high lakes.

A hundred and fifty years ago, ospreys were more common in Scotland. But so many were hunted and killed that each year fewer and fewer pairs built nests and raised baby birds. By the end of the nineteenth century there were only a handful of breeding pairs left. During the period between about 1910 and 1954, no ospreys at all were known to breed in the British Isles.

British ospreys died out for three reasons.

Firstly, they were
shot by gamekeepers
who were employed by
rich men to protect the
fish and game birds in their
rivers, lakes and grounds.
Secondly, they were shot by
collectors who wanted to have
them stuffed to put on display in
museums.   And thirdly, their big
white eggs with red blotches were
highly valued by egg collectors.

So for nearly fifty years, no
ospreys bred in the British Isles.
Then in 1954, one pair did breed,
and over the next twenty-five years
the numbers gradually increased.
In 1978 there were about twenty pairs.

That may not sound very many,
but that it happened at all was a
great triumph for the Royal Society for
the Protection of Birds.   The next story,
"Operation Osprey", is about that triumph.

8

Operation Osprey

When Philip Brown left the Air Force in 1946, he
joined the staff of the Royal Society for the
Protection of Birds. Soon afterwards, on a field
trip to Speyside in the Highlands of Scotland, he
met Desmond Nethersole Thompson, a brilliant
naturalist.

Desmond arrived late one evening at the small
hotel where Philip was staying. He was a big,
warm-hearted man, dedicated to protecting rare
birds from egg collectors and other dangers. Much
to Philip's surprise, Desmond said that he thought
that the osprey might soon start to breed again in
Britain, because he had seen one or two ospreys
passing the summer in Speyside.

This was exciting news, but that was all
Desmond would say. He was so secretive about it
that Philip began to wonder why. Was it possible
that a pair of ospreys had already returned to raise
chicks in Scotland?

The thick pine forests in Speyside make ideal
hiding places for rare birds. Deep in the forest
country, near the Cairngorm Mountains, there are
lakes called lochs and lochans, with fish to spare for
hungry ospreys. During the early 1950s, when

Philip became Secretary of the RSPB, he received reports from Desmond saying that single ospreys were still sometimes seen in the area. Then in 1955, a lucky bird-watcher spotted a pair of ospreys taking sticks to an old eyrie on a fir tree, in a high place called Sluggan Pass. *Eyrie* is the name of the huge nest built by a large bird of prey. The birds did not stay for long, because it was already summer and too late in the year for breeding.

Soon afterwards, an eyrie as big as a cartload of sticks was found, on top of a pine tree by the lonely shore of Loch Garten. Philip was thrilled when he saw it. He felt sure that ospreys must have bred there. But when? And did the chicks get away safely?

Then a letter signed by Desmond appeared in

The Scotsman newspaper. It said that a pair of Scottish ospreys had raised two chicks the year before, in 1954, but it did not say where their eyrie had been. Since Loch Garten was in Speyside — Desmond's home — Philip guessed that the ospreys must have bred in the old nest in the pine tree near the loch. But Desmond went on keeping his secret. He did not want any egg collectors to know just where ospreys were breeding in Britain for the first time in over forty years. If they knew, they would certainly try to rob the nest of the precious eggs.

During the spring of 1956, a watch was kept on both the Sluggan and Loch Garten nests, but no birds were seen there. This was the beginning of *Operation Osprey*, which became the name of the RSPB's efforts to help and protect the ospreys in Britain.

In May, Philip was called to Speyside by his friend George Waterston, to see where a pair of ospreys were starting to build an eyrie near Loch Morlich. The birds soon flew away, however, and both men were disappointed — until they heard some exciting news on the radio: Desmond had found a nest in the heart of the Speyside forest! He had even recorded the cries of one of the birds building it, and these sounds were broadcast by the

BBC.   Eggs were laid in the nest, but they were
destroyed by a hooded crow.

Operation Osprey really got going in 1957, when
the RSPB hired a skilled bird-watcher to patrol
Speyside, in search of ospreys and their nests.   As
it happened, it was a visitor to the forest who saw
the first osprey of 1957.

A bird was seen carrying an enormous stick —
about three centimetres thick and nearly a metre
long — to the old eyrie by Loch Garten.

When Philip heard about this, he thought that
the bird might be a male, back early from its
migration.   Perhaps if it found a mate, it might
breed.   He built a camp near the eyrie.   Then he
made arrangements for teams of volunteers to take
turns in watching the nest from a hiding place put
together from old sacking.   One lone bird was seen
a few times, then it flew away and was not seen
again that year.

After the exhausting and often boring work done by the teams of watchers, the departure of the osprey was a bitter blow. One man however — George Waterston — did not waste his time being miserable. Knowing by now that ospreys returned to their old eyries, he guessed that there was a strong chance that birds might go back to the Loch Garten nest in the next year, 1958. He started to plan a more comfortable base camp for *Operation Osprey*. He also arranged for more volunteers so that a twenty-four hour watch could be kept on the nest if the ospreys came.

The volunteers were ordinary people who cared a great deal about birds, and who gave up some of their holidays to help. They were given food and shelter (in tents and a caravan) by the RSPB, but

they were not paid any money for their unselfish work.

George Waterston's hunch proved right. On May Day 1958, a male osprey appeared, to be joined by a female three days later. Both birds began building up the huge nest of sticks, and lining it with grass, moss and heather. Everyone at the camp was happy, and the watchers settled down to their round-the-clock guard.

One day there was an excited shout: "The birds are up!" A high-pitched *pew-pew-pew-pew* sounded above the trees — the alarm call of an osprey. Somebody was approaching the eyrie through the forest, and a sudden intruder might frighten the birds away . . . . George let out a mighty yell. The intruder turned out to be only the local doctor's daughter, who had no idea that either the ospreys or the watchers were there!

The second intruder was far more dangerous. On a day soon after there should have been eggs in the nest, a man was seen wandering towards the eyrie. George gave his famous yell as he ran to the osprey tree, but the stranger got there first.

All George could do was to tell the man off and have him escorted back to his car, which was hidden in the forest. The man said that there was a single egg in the nest, but that he would never dream of taking the eggs of rare birds.

He was lying! When he gave his name, George recognised it as that of a well-known egg collector who would stop at nothing to possess such a special egg.

Through the summer the team watched. They found that the long hours between sunset and sunrise were the worst. Nights were cold, with frost and rain — and even the occasional snow shower. Mornings were misty. It could be very painful, sitting hunched up inside the hide near the eyrie. Using special binoculars by starlight, a watcher could just make out the head of an osprey sitting on the nest.

It was in the cold and wet early hours of the morning that Philip saw the shape of a man climbing up to the nest. He gave the alarm, but it was seconds too late. The man reached the nest, climbed down, and fled into the rain-soaked shadows.

By the light of day, the unhappy men of *Operation Osprey* found three smashed eggs. The now dead chicks had been just ready to hatch.

Success for *Operation Osprey* came in 1959. After the years of failure, George Waterston was a wiser man. Now he helped to make the Loch Garten area into a bird reserve. People going into it without permission could be fined.

He also had an old army field telephone wire put up, so that watchers in the hide could talk with their friends back at the base camp.

Ospreys appeared late in April, but after showing a little interest in the Loch Garten eyrie, they began to build a nest close by in the Abernethy Forest, which was part of the bird reserve. George and his volunteers had to rebuild the base camp, re-lay the telephone wire, and erect a new hiding place close to the new nest.

Nobody minded this extra work, because the ospreys were breeding again! Yet in those days, no one knew for sure whether the same ospreys were coming back each year to Speyside. This was because nobody wanted to risk catching an osprey to put an identity ring on its leg, in case the bird was scared away.

In 1959, three eggs were laid, and the female osprey spent most of her time brooding over them. The male bird went fishing several times each day. When he returned to the eyrie, he sat on a branch and ate part of the fish he had caught — before giving the female her share. Then he kept the eggs

warm while the female ate and "stretched her legs".
The eggs hatched after thirty-eight days. Now
that the female had chicks to look after, the male
let her eat her share of the fish first, and give pieces
to the young birds, before he flew off with his share.

It was about this time that George had what
Philip Brown thought at first was a mad idea.
Why not build a public viewing place behind the
hide, and allow people to come and see the osprey
family through telescopes and binoculars? After
this news was announced by the BBC that summer,
fourteen thousand people went to watch the ospreys
at a rate of three hundred a day. And George was

waiting there to collect funds for the work of the RSPB!

George Waterston's "peep-show", as Philip called it, can now be seen every year at the Loch Garten bird reserve, near Aviemore. Ospreys have bred at the eyrie there most years since 1959. If the well-meaning Desmond had not been so secretive in the early days, perhaps the RSPB might have been able to help the ospreys sooner. But that does not matter now, because each year more than twenty pairs of ospreys are breeding in various parts of Britain.

Today the RSPB is richer in funds, and can afford to use electronic warning devices and listening microphones in the war against vandals and egg collectors. The fight to protect Britain's wild life must go on. We can only win if everybody cares enough about nature to support the work of caring people like Philip, George, Desmond — and those unselfish people who gave up their holidays to help.

The Man Who Made a Vacuum

When you go on a picnic, you probably take a flask of hot tea or coffee with you. And even after several hours, your drink will still be piping hot. Have you ever wondered why this is? It is because your flask is a *vacuum* flask.

It has two walls of thin glass (some modern ones are of metal), rather like a small bottle fitted inside a slightly larger one. In between the two walls there is a space with no air in it. This space is empty — in other words, it is a *vacuum*.

Where else will you find a vacuum? There is one in an electric light bulb — it has no air, just a little helium gas. In shops you will see tins of coffee marked "vacuum packed" — the coffee is stored in a vacuum so that it stays fresh. And outer space is also a vacuum, for it is almost empty.

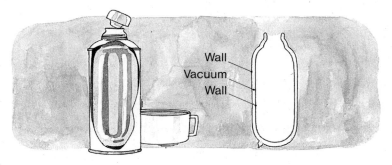

Wall
Vacuum
Wall

Perhaps the first person to make a vacuum was a German engineer called Otto von Guericke, who was born in Magdeburg in Germany almost four hundred years ago. As a young man, he travelled in England and France, as well as Germany. Later he became a soldier, fighting in several battles and working as an engineer in the army. Then at last he went back to his home town, where he had time to think about his favourite subject, science.

At that time, scientists thought it was impossible to make a vacuum. Otto was sure they were wrong, and he decided to prove it.

He started by making a brass pump which would suck air or water out of containers. It worked like a bicycle pump in reverse. When the handle was pulled, the air or water was sucked *up* the tube, rather than pushed down it.

Otto fitted the pump to a wine-cask filled with water. He tried to fix it as firmly as possible, using brass bands and iron screws to hold it in place. Then he was ready to begin.

He pulled and pulled on the pump, trying to get all the water out of the cask. But before he managed this, the brass bands and the iron screws gave way. They were not strong enough for the job.

He tried again, using stronger bands and screws. This time they stayed in place, but Otto found that he could not pump all the water out on his own. Three other men had to help him.

In the end they managed to pump nearly all the water out of the cask, and there was nothing left except a little water and a lot of empty space.

At this point they heard a strange bubbling noise. It sounded almost as if the water left inside was boiling — but that was impossible, for the cask was cold. What was happening?

Otto found that air was leaking into the cask through the joins in the wood. Soon it was full of air, just like an ordinary empty wine-cask.

"This is no good," thought Otto. "I need a container that won't leak." So for his next experiment he used a large copper globe. He filled it with water, and fixed his pump to a tube coming out of the globe. This time two men pumped away until they could hardly move the handle.

Then suddenly, there was a loud bang — so loud that all three men were terrified by the noise. At the same moment, they saw the copper globe crumple up like a squashed paper bag.

Otto did not know why it had collapsed. In fact, it was the air pressing upon the outside of the globe. When all the water had been drawn out of the globe, there was nothing inside to resist the pressure of the air, and so the globe collapsed. (This is called an *implosion*.)

He tried yet again, and made a much stronger and heavier globe. He made another improvement as well, fixing a tap on the tube from the globe to the pump. This time he managed to empty all the air from the globe without it collapsing. He turned the tap to shut off the air, and removed the pump. Inside the globe was a vacuum!

Then Otto did something rather brave. He stepped forward, put his hand on the tap, and turned it on. Immediately there was a loud whistling as air rushed in to fill the empty globe. Otto stepped back quickly. Even from several metres away, he could feel the rush of air! He was lucky. If his hand had been anywhere near the end of the tube, it could have been sucked in, and he might have been badly hurt.

Unaware perhaps of the danger, Otto was happy with his success. His next step was to make a pump specially for pumping out air instead of water. With this, he tried several different experiments with a vacuum inside a glass globe.

First he put a loudly ticking clock inside the globe. He began to pump the air out and as he pumped, the ticking of the clock became fainter and fainter. In the end, when there was no air left in the globe, he could not hear the ticking at all. But he knew the clock was still going, because through the glass he could see the hands moving.

His next experiment was with a lighted candle inside the globe. As he drew the air out, he watched the candle closely. Quite suddenly the flame began to flicker and then went out. A flame needs oxygen to burn, and once the air was sucked out there was no oxygen left.

Later he placed grapes, fresh for eating, in a glass bottle, and drew out the air. They stayed fresh in the vacuum for six months, with no sign of rotting or decay. We still use this method to keep coffee and other things fresh.

One day Otto made what is now his most famous test. He decided to find out just how strong a vacuum is — or rather, how strong is the force of the air that presses down on us. This test was one of the most exciting that scientists have ever made.

Out of copper, he made two half globes, like two hollow cups. He made them exactly similar, so that they fitted together to form a perfect globe, thirty-six centimetres across. He put a small tube onto one of the half globes, then one of his men held the two halves together while Otto pumped out

all the air.   When he had finished, the two half globes were held together as solidly as if they had been bolted together.   Yet the only thing holding them together was the pressure of air.   Otto could not pull the two halves apart, even with the strongest men helping him.

He decided to use these half globes to show the world the power of a vacuum.   In 1654, he announced that he was going to try to pull the globes apart with two teams of horses.   The test was to be in the park of the German Emperor's palace, and Otto took his copper globe, his pump — and sixteen huge carthorses, harnessed in two teams of eight.   One team of horses was fastened with chains to one half of the globe, and one team to the other half.

The Emperor was watching, and at a signal from him, the two teams of horses were driven away from each other. It was like a giant tug-of-war, except that the horses were trying to pull the globe apart!

The two teams strained on their harnesses, sweating. The chains were stretched tight.

A hush fell on the watching crowd as the horses pulled harder and harder. Suddenly, with a loud crack, the globe came apart, and the crowd cheered. Otto had shown that the air presses on everything very strongly indeed.

Otto made many other experiments, and wrote seven large books on vacuums. Other people continued his experiments, and now we use vacuums in many different ways — from television tubes to vacuum cleaners.

We can also use them for fun. Here is a toy that Otto invented, called the diver.

Find a soft plastic see-through bottle or an ordinary glass bottle with a soft plastic top. Fill it with water — right up to the top. Put a "diver" — an orange pip will do, for example — in the bottle and fasten the top on tightly. Now, when you squeeze the bottle or press the lid, the little diver should sink to the bottom. When you lift your finger off the top, the diver will rise again.

The secret lies in the bubbles of air that cling to the diver. When you press on the bottle, you increase the pressure, the bubbles of air become smaller and the diver sinks. When you lift off your finger or stop squeezing the bottle, the air bubbles grow larger again and the diver rises.

How to Walk on the Ceiling

Inside the theatre, it was dark. Only the stage was brightly lit. On it, a slight, pretty girl with long dark hair walked slowly and carefully along a highly-polished wooden board. As she took each delicate step, the audience clapped and cheered. What was so clever about that? you may ask. She was Aimee the Human Fly — and she was upside down!

There were big round suction cups on the soles of Aimee's special shoes. As she pressed each foot against the board, the air under the cups was squeezed out. This meant that the air all around the suckers would force them to stick to the board to hold her weight. She had to move slowly, in little steps, ten centimetres at a time.

If you have a small suction cup at home (the kind that is used to clear a blocked kitchen sink), try pushing it down very hard against a smooth table. Then pull. Feel how the air presses down all round, to make it stick. Now see if you can find a place where the sucker will stick upside down.

The Man who Loved Engines

The first great man of the railway age was George Stephenson. He was born to poor parents in the north of England over two hundred years ago, in 1781. Even as a child he was interested in engines; he used to make clay models of the steam engines near his home. At that time these engines were used to pump water out of coal mines, and to haul the coal to the surface.

George's parents were too poor to pay the one and a half pence needed to send him to school, and he was eighteen before he learned to read and write. Whilst still a boy, he started work at the pit where his father was employed as a fireman (the fireman shovelled coal to provide steam for the pumping machine).

First of all George drove one of the horses, and then became a picker (picking stones and dross out of the coal).

Mine workers moved from pit to pit, because when a mine was worked out, it was closed. So each time his father had to move, George went with him, to work at the new pit. He did several jobs at the different mines, but he was always interested in engines. He spent all his spare time working on them, and came to know more and more about them.

When he was fourteen, he became assistant fireman to his father. Although it was not his job, he often took the pump engine to pieces after his work was over, then put it together again.

When that pit closed, George got a job at another pit as fireman in his own right. Now he was interested in all the machinery in the mine, not only the pumps. Because he knew so much about it, he was often asked to mend machines when they broke down.

By the time he was seventeen, he was a good enough engineer to be put in charge of a pumping machine in a Northumberland coal mine.

Then one day in 1811, an important pumping machine broke down in a mine where George was working. The owners of the mine were worried, because the mine was flooded and the men could not go down to work. None of the expert engineers could mend the machine, but George was bold enough to say that he could do it.

The mine owners were too worried to care that he was not a properly trained engineer, and they gave George his chance. He mended the pumping engine — and was at once put in charge of it! The first thing he did then was to raise the pressure of steam, to make the machine work better. (Water was heated in a boiler and turned into steam, which drove the wheels of the machine. The more powerful the steam, the better the machine worked.) George made that engine work so well that it scared everyone by almost shaking the pumping house apart!

By now he was an important man, with a good house and a horse and gig to ride about in. But he still thought of himself as a working man, and never tried to show off. So none of his workmates minded his well-deserved success.

Up to now, George Stephenson had worked on the stationary steam engines used in the pits for pumping water and bringing men and coal to the surface. He had however seen them used for another purpose, and it gave his thoughts a different direction.

Horses were always used to haul the heavy trucks of coal to the ships which carried it south to London and other places. There were few roads, and most of those were very rough, so wooden tracks were laid to make the job easier. Since the wooden tracks soon splintered and wore out, they were later lined with iron plates that had bent-up sides, to stop the trucks from running into the mud. They were called horse tramways, and in some ways they were the very first railways.

In one place near where George Stephenson lived, the trucks were hauled up the hills by stationary steam engines, and allowed to run down the other side. On level ground, horses were still used.

This system was faster and easier than the old way of doing it, but George thought it could be made better yet. He looked at the horse tramways and dreamed of replacing them with solid iron lines. And he dreamed of using *moving* steam engines, instead of slowly plodding horses.

With the help of his son Robert, his dreams were to come true. Since George had never gone to school, he knew — better than most people — just how important it could be. So he sent Robert to the village school, and later to a good school in Newcastle.

At the end of each day, when Robert returned after a long ride home on a donkey, he talked with his father about the things he was learning. He talked about the new ideas in mathematics and science, and George listened carefully, learning the new things too.

George was still working in a coal mine, but he did not forget his dreams of iron lines and moving steam engines. Slowly other people began to share those dreams and to be interested in those ideas. It became more and more expensive to keep horses, but George knew that he could build an engine that would be cheaper to run than keeping a horse.

At last he was given his chance. A mine owner asked him to build a locomotive to work on the old horse tramway that ran from his pit to the river.

George Stephenson's first locomotive was named the *Blucher*. The *Blucher*'s most important feature was its flanged wheels. The flanges, or raised inner edges, locked on to the tram lines just as the wheels of railway trucks do today. This meant that the lines no longer needed the costly raised sides.

The main trouble with the *Blucher* was that it kept losing steam pressure, which meant that it kept stopping. It was driven by George's older brother James, and one day it broke down as it was passing his house. He shouted to his wife Jinnie to come and help him. She was a strong woman and together they got the *Blucher* started again — by pushing! Jinnie used to get up at four o'clock every workday morning, to light the *Blucher*'s fire.

By 1821, George had become well known as an expert on building locomotives for the short-distance hauls on the tramways. His dream however was still to build much longer railways, and more

Flange

powerful locomotives — and again he got his chance!

He was chosen to survey the possible route, and to work out the cost, of a railway to be built between the coal mines around Darlington and the town of Stockton on the river Tees. He chose his son Robert to be his chief assistant.

The Stockton and Darlington Railway was to be more than fifty kilometres long: much longer than any other railway at that time. It was also new in another way. It was going to be a public line, which meant that it would also carry passengers. The owners wanted to use horses to pull the trucks,

but George wanted them to use locomotives. In
the end, both were used.

Building the railway gave George and Robert an
opportunity to learn the work of civil engineers.
Just as civil engineers have to do, they had to dig
cuttings through low hills and build up banks of
earth, to carry the railway line. The line had to be
as level as possible because the locomotives were
not powerful enough to pull heavy trucks up steep
slopes. George and Robert also built bridges over
rivers.

The first locomotive engines for the Stockton and
Darlington Railway were made in the world's first

locomotive works in Newcastle. They were
designed and built by George Stephenson, and the
first one was named *Locomotion*.

It worked like this. Its big upright steam tubes,
or cylinders, were fixed inside a huge boiler, to
make steam. When the steam was at high pressure,
it forced pistons up and down inside the cylinders.
The pistons worked levers which were joined to the
connecting rods that linked the two wheels on each
side of the engine. *Locomotion* could travel at
between twenty and twenty-four kilometres an
hour — the speed of a galloping horse. It was a
great improvement on the *Blucher*.

The 27th of September 1825 was a proud day for the Stephensons. Music played and cannons roared for the opening of the world's first public railway.

First came a horseman with a flag. Then came George himself, driving puffing, clanking *Locomotion*, pulling thirty trucks filled with six hundred cheering people!

Even before the Stockton and Darlington Railway was finished, George Stephenson began work on another railway. This one was to join Liverpool to Manchester, two of the great new industrial cities of the north of England. This time he had trouble with the rich men who owned the land over which

the railway would go. They said that the trains would be noisy and spoil their fox-hunting. Sometimes George's workmen were even attacked with hay forks and shotguns.

The next problem was that the railway had to go across a wide swamp called Chat Moss. The ground was so soft that workmen had to wear boards on their feet to stop them from sinking. Earth and stones just sank in the marsh.

Other engineers said that it was impossible to build a railway across Chat Moss. By now, however, George was an expert civil engineer, and he knew how to deal with this problem. He ordered his men to build a long floating raft of

wood and branches across the swamp. The railway was laid on top of this.

When the railway had been built, the owners offered a prize of £500 for the engineer who built the fastest locomotive. Of course this interested George very much, so he and Robert set to work.

They built an engine called the *Rocket*, with a new kind of boiler made with many strong iron tubes. Heating water in these tubes meant that the *Rocket* could keep up a steady high pressure of steam, and this made the new engine powerful. Other people built engines, and in 1829 a great competition was held at Rainhill, near Liverpool, to decide which was best. Ten thousand people turned up to cheer!

There were five engines taking part — one of them actually had a horse inside it, instead of a boiler! And, with a cloud of white steam puffing from its tall chimney, the yellow and black painted *Rocket* was the winner!

In the years that followed, both George and Robert took their places amongst the great men who helped to create Britain's network of railways, but George never forgot the day he won the Rainhill Trials. It was the finest moment in his life!

Drilling an Oil Well

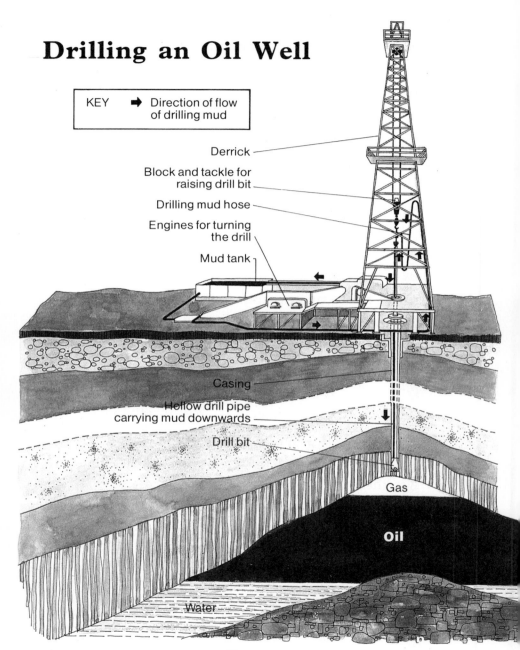

KEY ➡ Direction of flow of drilling mud

Derrick

Block and tackle for raising drill bit

Drilling mud hose

Engines for turning the drill

Mud tank

Casing

Hollow drill pipe carrying mud downwards

Drill bit

Gas

Oil

Water

Oil is very important in the modern world. It is used in industry to make many chemicals, as well as petrol.

To find oil, which lies deep under the ground, the oil men have to set up a drilling rig and drill down through the layers of rock. First they set up a derrick, like the one shown, with a block and tackle to control the drilling *bit*. The bit turns at high speed, and has jagged teeth to cut through the rock and earth. When it wears out, the oil men raise it by means of the block and tackle, and change it.

Fixed to the bit is a double tube called the drill pipe. Mud is pumped down the inside tube, and this pushes the pieces of rock up through the outer tube. The rock and mud pumped up is then separated — the rock is examined for signs of oil and the mud is re-used.

When the bit first cuts through to the oil, it gushes up with great force, covering the workers from head to foot!

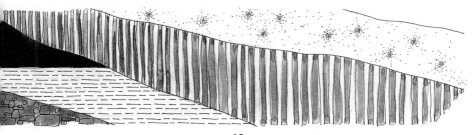

The X-ray Man

Some of the greatest discoveries in the world have been made just by chance, when a scientist was working on something quite different. This was how X-rays were discovered.

Nearly everyone has had an X-ray photograph (properly called a *radiograph*) taken at some time or other — in a hospital to check if a bone has been broken, or at the dentist's to make sure that a new tooth is growing in straight. And if you have ever

44

flown from a big airport, your hand baggage may have been checked by X-ray — for these rays can be used to see through more than skin. They can see through wood, and paper, and cloth, and most types of metal. They are used to test weaknesses in metal structures, and even to check if a painting is a forgery or not.

So X-rays are very important to all sorts of people, and they were discovered — by accident — by a German professor, Wilhelm Röntgen, in 1895.

One day, he was doing some experiments with a Crookes' tube — this was a big glass tube similar to a modern television tube. The air had been drawn out of it, so that there was a *vacuum* inside. The tube also contained two metal plates. As the professor started on his next experiment, he fastened these plates to a battery, in order to pass an electric current through the completely empty space between the two plates.

As soon as the current flowed, the professor saw that one of the plates was glowing slightly. He had never noticed this happening before, and he was interested. He darkened the room where he was working, then he put black paper round the Crookes' tube so that he could see the strange glow more clearly.

Sure enough, an eerie, greenish light was coming from one of the plates — but it was not the only glow! On a nearby bench there was a piece of glass covered with a special chemical called barium salt. This had nothing to do with the experiment he was working on. It was not connected to the tube in any way at all — but it too was glowing. It was glowing even though there was thick black paper between it and the Crookes' tube.

As he examined this strange effect, Professor Röntgen grew more and more interested. He looked round the room for a thick book, and placed it between the front of the tube and the glass covered with barium salt. The piece of glass still glowed! Next he found a block of wood, and then a sheet of aluminium, to put between the tube and the piece of glass. Neither of these made any difference at all to the green glow. The piece of glass went on glowing even when he put his hand in the way.

Wilhelm Röntgen thought about what had happened, and decided that the tube was giving out rays like radio waves, but since he did not know what sort of rays they were, he called them X-rays. (To a scientist, "X" means something unknown.) He couldn't work out *why* these things were happening, but he went on trying more and more experiments. He found that the only thing which seemed to stop the X-rays was a sheet of lead.

Then he tried an experiment with a photographic plate. (Films as we know them today did not then exist. Photographs were taken on glass plates, one by one.) He wrapped the plate in black paper, and left it by the tube for some hours. When he opened it, the photographic plate was fogged — as if light had been shining on it. But there had been no light; only the X-rays.

After this, Professor Röntgen found that he could photograph objects with X-rays. He put a coin in front of another well-wrapped photographic plate, and left the two things in front of the Crookes' tube.

When he developed the plate, he found that he
had a photograph of the outline of the coin. The
same thing worked with a key and a chain. Finally,
he took a photograph of his wife's hand. This one
showed not only the ring on her third finger, but
also the outline of the bones of her hand.

At last he decided to tell other scientists about
his great discovery, and he wrote down all the
experiments he had done, with the results that he
had achieved.

But it was so important a discovery that soon the
whole world knew, not only the scientists. First to
recognise the enormous value of X-rays were
doctors; for the first time they could see inside a
living body. They could X-ray a broken leg, and
see exactly which bones were broken and where.

They could see just where to put a splint on a broken bone to help it to mend.

Later, doctors discovered that X-rays could help to cure some serious diseases as well.

X-rays were also useful in science. They were used to explore the atom, for example, and this led over the years to the discovery of nuclear energy, which can generate electricity to light our homes and power modern submarines; as well as make the atom bomb.

Professor Wilhelm Röntgen knew that his lucky discovery was important, but he could not have even dreamed of the effects it was going to have in medicine and science from that time forward.

Useful X-rays

Did you know that X-rays have revealed hidden paintings? X-rays have also been used to reveal the name of the painter.

Not long ago, an oil painting of two men came into the hands of art experts. They thought the painting was probably done by the famous Italian artist, Titian. Titian lived and worked in the sixteenth century.

1 Before cleaning   2 After cleaning

But the experts could not be sure that he had painted the picture. They only suspected that it was by Titian. So they decided to try to find out if there was a name hidden underneath the paint.

They had the painting cleaned and a third head was revealed as you can see in picture 2. The art experts were so excited by their discovery that they decided to find out more about the painting.

So they had an X-ray picture taken of it. The X-rays went through the top layer of oil paint and revealed below it another layer of paint. They discovered that there was another portrait painted on the canvas. As you can see, the figure in the middle looks to the left of the picture; the other painting showed him looking to the right. The X-rays also revealed that the portrait of the three men was indeed painted by Titian.

The First Aeroplane

The next time you see an aeroplane overhead, or fly
in one, think how amazing it is that it stays up in
the sky. These great, heavy machines are held up
by thin air. Today we hardly think about the
marvel of flight and planes take off and land at big
airports such as London at the rate of over seven
hundred a day. They travel high into the thin
atmosphere above the earth, and many fly at speeds
of over 1600 kilometres an hour. So it seems
strange to think of a time when there were no
planes at all in the sky — but it is less than a
hundred years since the first petrol-driven aeroplane
flew. That first flight lasted only twelve seconds.
The plane travelled just thirty-six metres, going
about as fast as most of us can run.

It all started with two young Americans, Wilbur
and Orville Wright. All their lives the Wright
brothers were fascinated by machines, and even as
boys they were interested in flying. They made
and flew toy helicopters — to the great annoyance
of their family. They were interested in printing,
too, and when Orville was a teenager he built his
own printing press. With Wilbur he launched a

weekly newspaper in their home town, Dayton, Ohio: Wilbur wrote the paper and Orville printed it.

Then when Wilbur was twenty-one and his brother twenty-five, they became interested in another new machine: the safety bicycle. There were no motor cars at that time, and people had to walk or ride on horseback. The bicycle changed all that. It offered a cheap, fast way of getting from place to place. When the Wright brothers realised just how popular it was going to be, they set up their own cycle shop. At first they simply sold and repaired bicycles, but soon they began making and selling their own make of bicycle, called the *Flyer*.

All this time they had kept up their early interest in flying. They read every book on flight that they could get hold of, and Wilbur spent hours watching birds as they flew.

Best of all he liked to watch buzzards. He watched these great birds of prey for hours on end, seeing how they flew. He saw how they flapped their wings very little, soaring and gliding on the air, swooping from side to side by twisting their wing tips. He was to use what he saw when he came to make his first aeroplane.

* * * * * *

Early in 1899, a famous glider inventor called Otto
Lilienthal was killed flying one of his own gliders.
Surprisingly, perhaps, that made the Wright
brothers keen to build their own glider.

Wilbur said to his brother,

"Why don't we build a safety glider that won't
crash?" — and they finished their first glider only a
few months later, in August 1899. It was small,
only one and a half metres from wingtip to wingtip,
and of course it could not carry people. But it did
show them that it would be possible to build and
fly a larger machine.

So the next machine was much bigger — big
enough to carry one of the brothers. It was five
metres from wingtip to wingtip, and it had another

small wing that stuck out in front. The Wright brothers called this a "rudder" because, like the rudder on a boat, it helped to control the direction in which the plane flew. Other gliders would fly straight for a while and then suddenly slip sideways. If the pilot was not careful (or lucky!), the sideslip could lead to a crash. Wilbur thought back to how buzzards swooped from side to side in the air by twisting their wings, and he worked out a way of twisting the wings of the glider to control the direction of the flight.

They tried their new glider near Dayton, but the winds there were changeable, which made flying difficult. They needed a place with strong, steady winds to do their tests.

Kitty Hawk, about 900 kilometres away on the coast of North Carolina, had winds of the right sort. They moved their glider to the lonely sand-dunes there, and set up camp.

To get the glider into the air, one of the brothers had to run along, pulling the glider by a rope fixed to its nose. The other brother was the pilot. He had to lie flat on his stomach to cut down wind resistance, and pull on cords fixed to the wings to control the glider in the air. As always, Orville and Wilbur took it in turns to fly. At first they

found it difficult to take off. The glider used to
tip over on one wing. So the brothers asked a
friend from the nearby lifeboat station to help them.
He held on to the wingtip to stop the glider tipping
over.

As it was only a glider, they did not fly very
far that year, but they were pleased with the way
it worked. They went home to Dayton to make a
bigger and better one.

The next year they were back at Kitty Hawk with
another glider. More flights and more tests
followed but still they had not found a way to
control the glider properly. Again they went back
to Dayton to work at the problem of finding the
right shape of wing. They could not afford to
test every wing shape by building a new glider
so they built a small wind tunnel in their cycle
shop. This was a wooden tube about twelve metres
across, with a fan at one end that blew air through
the tube. They tested different wing shapes in
the tunnel and found that the best shape was
slightly humped — like a bridge.

They built a new glider with this wing shape
and by 1903 it was ready for testing. Again they
took it to Kitty Hawk. Again they spent weeks
making test flights. This time the glider was a

complete success. They made almost a thousand flights in it — with not one crash. Wilbur and Orville had only one problem left to solve — how to steer the glider. They still had their "rudder" at the front of the plane, but because it was fixed level with the ground and not upright it could not be used to steer the glider.

All one night Orville lay awake thinking about the steering. By morning he had the answer. He put the "rudder" at the back of the glider rather than at the front and he set it upright — like the tailfin of a fish. Then he fastened cords to it so that the pilot would be able to control both the rudder and the wings at the same time. The new rudder worked perfectly and the brothers found they could control their glider as well as a bird flies.

Once they had built their "safety" glider the Wright brothers began work on an aircraft with a propeller and an engine. The engine was not too difficult but the propeller was much harder. Although propellers had been used on boats nobody knew what a propeller for an aircraft should be like.

All through the long hot summer of 1903 they worked in their cycle shop. By September they had what they needed: a small, light petrol engine and two propellers — one to go behind each wing.

The engine weighed about a hundred kilograms and was about as powerful as a small car engine. Their glider now had an engine and two propellers to push it through the air.

"We'll call it the *Flyer* after our bicycle," Wilbur said. Orville happily agreed.

Back they went to Kitty Hawk to test it out. Things went wrong from the start. The *Flyer* kept breaking down and it wasn't until the twelfth of December 1903 that they were ready to take off. Then bad weather stopped them and they had to wait yet another two days.

At last, on the fourteenth of December, the
weather was just right.   The two brothers tested
the wind direction and checked their runway.
Two wooden rails, twelve metres long, ran down
the hill facing *into* the wind.   A little wheeled
truck rested on the rails and on top of the truck sat
the *Flyer*.   And now — would it live up to its
name and fly?

The wind was blowing strong and steady over the
dunes and in the right direction, up the rails.   The
brothers tossed a coin to see who should go first.
Wilbur won, and he grinned at his brother as he lay
down in the *Flyer*.   Orville started the engine and
the propellers whirred round.   Orville let go the
rope holding back the plane and the *Flyer* slid along
the rails, gathering speed down the slope.

At the end of the rails, Wilbur felt the plane
lift up into the air.   For a moment he was airborne,
but the *Flyer* rose too steeply and it lost speed.
The nose dropped and the plane crashed into the
soft sand.   Wilbur stepped out unhurt, but the
wooden struts of the plane were cracked and
broken.   Orville ran over to him.

"I didn't steer it properly," Wilbur shouted
angrily to his brother.   "That's why it crashed."

Three days later the *Flyer* was mended and ready

for another trial. This time they laid the rails
on flat ground so that the *Flyer* had to take off
under its own power. It was Orville's turn to go
first and at ten thirty on the morning of the
seventeenth of December he took off. This time
there were no accidents. Orville took the plane
up to a height of three metres and held it level
there. He was flying into the teeth of a winter
gale, but still managed a speed of sixteen
kilometres an hour. The Wright brothers had
done it. In all, Orville flew twelve seconds and
covered a distance of thirty-six metres through
the air.

Two more flights — first by Wilbur, then Orville
— and then, the last flight of the day. Wilbur took
off from the rails, and soon had the little *Flyer*
under control. The ground was sliding along
underneath him briskly, and the wind was whistling

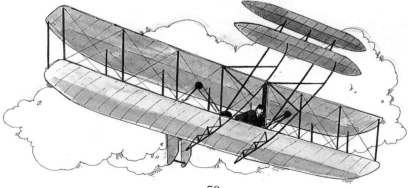

in his ears. When a little hummock of sand appeared in front of him, he pulled on the controls and the plane responded beautifully, rising up and over the sand dune.

But Wilbur felt that he was now a little too high off the ground for safety, so he pulled the cords and the plane's nose dipped. Before he could correct his mistake, the machine's skids had touched the ground, and the flight was over.

All the same, he had been in the air for fifty-nine

seconds — their longest yet — and had flown nearly
260 metres. Wilbur climbed out of the *Flyer* and
said to Orville, "The age of the flying machine is
here at last."

It was too late in the year to make many other
flights, so they packed up camp and returned to
Dayton. There they made a second and a third
Flyer, both better than the first.

Now that their machine had an engine, a strong
steady wind was no longer important, and they
could try out the new plane near their home at
Dayton. They flew it all through the summer of
1905 in a large field called Huffman Prairie, and in
all they made forty-nine test flights.

In time they learned to control the new aeroplane
perfectly. First they found that a weight of
twenty-five kilograms in the front of the plane
stopped the nose bobbing up and down. Next they
realised that they could carry a passenger instead of
the weight. They learned to bank, to fly in a circle,
and even to fly in a figure of eight. On one flight
they stayed up in the air for half an hour.

Although newspaper reporters came to see the
Flyer, they were not very interested in it. Airships
were already flying much further and staying up in
the air much longer than the little plane. Nor was the

American government interested. They took three years even to decide to look at this new machine.

But if governments weren't interested, ordinary people were. All over America and Europe, they were keen to see the flying machines. In 1908 Wilbur took a new aeroplane to France. He made over a hundred flights there, the longest one lasting two hours and twenty minutes. He took up over sixty passengers, and not once did he have an accident.

Back in America, Orville was flying just as brilliantly as his brother in France. He also took up many passengers but, unlike Wilbur, he *did* have an accident, although it was not his fault.

It happened when he was trying to sell the *Flyer* to the American government, who had at last shown some interest. An Army officer had come to fly as a passenger, to see if the machine could be useful to the Army. They took off smoothly, but while they were in the air one of the propeller blades split. It tore away the wing, and the rudder broke off. Orville could do nothing to prevent a crash, in which the Army man was killed and Orville himself was injured.

It was the only accident that the Wrights ever had, and because of it the United States Army refused to buy the plane. It was too dangerous, they said.

In time Orville recovered from the accident, and the next year he went to France to join Wilbur. Everywhere they went in Europe, the brothers were met by cheering crowds who flocked to watch their "show flights". After a while, Orville went back to America, leaving Wilbur to continue the show flights in Europe.

Again Orville tried to sell a new aeroplane to the United States Army, and this time they were interested. They bought the machine, and soon Wright machines were being built in Britain, France and Germany as well as in America.

Soon after those years of success, Wilbur died. Orville retired in 1915, but he continued to work on his aircraft — still in the shop at Dayton where they had built their first machines.

He lived on until 1948, so that he saw just how much aircraft changed in those thirty years after his first successful flight. Other men worked on improving the ideas of the Wright brothers, and soon aeroplanes were flying higher, faster and further than the two men had ever dreamed. But it all started on that windy December morning in 1903, with that first twelve-second flight.

Making a Paper Aeroplane

The Wright brothers had great trouble keeping their aeroplanes flying straight and stopping them from stalling — that is, tipping up and nose-diving. You can study these problems by making a paper aeroplane and flying it.

To make a good aeroplane, take a sheet of paper about 21 cm wide by 30 cm long (A4 size).

1 Fold the long edge of the sheet up about 1.5 cm. Fold it again and again, five times in all. Now you should have a sheet about 14 cm wide and still 30 cm long, with a flattened roll of paper along the long edge, as shown in picture 1.

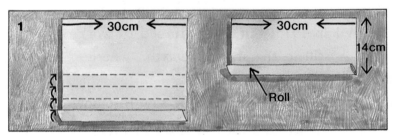

2 Now fold the paper in half so that the short edges meet (picture 2).

3 Crease the fold well and turn down both ends (these are the wings of your plane) to make a "V" in the middle (see picture 3). It looks like a bird now. The "V" should be about 1.5 cm deep.

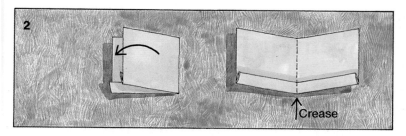

Crease

4 Fold the ends of the wings up by about 1.5 cm (see picture 4). This will help the aeroplane to fly straight.

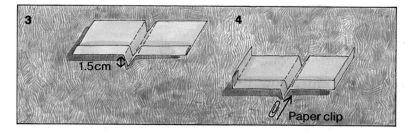

1.5cm

Paper clip

Finally, fix a paper clip to the front edge of the "V", where the flattened roll of paper is. This is to stop it stalling. You may need to use two paper clips.

Now the aeroplane is ready. See how far you can get it to glide in a straight line and without stalling. You may need to alter the wing tips and the number of paper clips — just as the Wright brothers had to alter the shape of their early aeroplanes.

The Man Who Invented Radio

Press a button — and there's the music you like best. Press another button, and the news comes through, from a city hundreds of kilometres away. Turn the dial, and you can hear a foreign language from a far country. That's radio — still called "wireless" by many older people — and it has been part of our everyday lives for generations.

As you tune in to your favourite programme, do you ever wonder just how it is that you can hear those sounds? How do they travel through the air and reach your radio, clear and intact, exactly as they are sent out?

It all began nearly a hundred years ago, when a young Italian called Guglielmo Marconi discovered how to send sounds through the air.

Marconi was born in Bologna, in northern Italy, in 1874. His father was a wealthy Italian

businessman, and his mother was a Scot who had lived in Ireland and had gone to Italy to study music. The family lived in a country house, the Villa Grifone, just outside Bologna.

As a boy, Marconi was not thought to be particularly clever. He was a quiet boy who spoke little but thought a lot. He liked nothing better than to sit and read science books in his father's big library. He also loved to do experiments with electricity, and he was always making electrical gadgets. For most of his early life, he was taught at home; he did not go to school.

Marconi was just twenty years old when the idea of making a radio first came to him. He was on holiday in the Italian mountains when a famous scientist called Hertz died. In a newspaper article young Marconi read about the experiments Hertz had done with strange electrical waves that went through the air.

"These waves could be used to send *sounds* through the air," Marconi thought to himself excitedly. "Why, with these waves, people could talk to each other over great distances, without wires."

Nobody before had thought of using these wireless waves to send sounds through the air, although several people had studied them. But the young Marconi was sure it could be done, and from that moment forward he thought of nothing else.

He gave up his holiday and went straight back to the Villa Grifone. There, in the attic where he had his own small laboratory, Marconi set to work to make wireless waves.

He started by repeating all Hertz's experiments. Hertz had found that a spark sent out these electric waves. He found too that these waves could make another small spark jump across a small gap in a loop of wire held a few metres away. Marconi decided to take the idea further. He was going to make the second spark *do* something. He was going to turn it into an electric current. First he built a transmitter to send out sparks. When

he tapped a Morse key a spark flew between two large brass spheres.

Then Marconi set up his *receiver* at the other end of the attic, to pick up the wireless waves. He fixed up a metal cylinder and joined it with wire to a special tube filled with metal filings of silver and nickel. This tube was called a *coherer*, and it turned the spark for the wireless waves into a small steady electric current, like the one you would get from a torch battery. He joined the coherer with wire to several glass jars with metal foil in them. He had used his mother's fruit bottling jars, but now they were being used to store electricity.

Next he joined the jars to an electric doorbell, and lastly, he joined the tubes, jars and doorbell to an electric battery, and his receiver was complete.

Marconi took the whole autumn to make and put together his transmitter and receiver, and only then was he ready to start his experiments. His idea was to get the spark from the brass spheres to send out the wireless waves to his receiver, which would turn them into an electric current and ring the doorbell. No one else had ever tried such an experiment.

For several months his experiments were unsuccessful. Then one freezing night in December 1894, he tapped the Morse key, a spark flew between the brass spheres — and the bell rang on the other side of the attic!

Forgetting how late it was, he ran downstairs to his mother's room and knocked on the door. "Mother, Mother!" he called excitedly. "Wake up!"

His mother rose sleepily and, putting on a dressing-gown, followed her son upstairs to his attic laboratory. There he tried to tell her what he had discovered.

"Look, mother, this is the transmitter," he said, pointing to the Morse key and the brass spheres. Then he led her to the other side of the attic. "And here is the receiver," he said, pointing to the large cylinder and the glass jars.

"What are those fruit jars doing?" asked his mother.

"Oh, those are for storing electricity now," her son replied. "They are part of my receiver," he added proudly. "Look, Mother," he went on, "do you see, there are no wires joining the Morse key to the bell!"

His mother looked, and nodded her head, still puzzled.

"Now listen," said Marconi, walking back to the Morse key. He pressed it — a spark flew — and the bell rang.

Mrs Marconi was astonished. "How does it work? I don't understand," she said.

"It's a bit hard to explain, Mother," said Marconi, "but do you see what it means?"

His mother had no idea, and said so.

"It means," went on Marconi, "that I can send messages through the air by Morse code, without any wires. And since there are no wires, I'm going to call it a 'wireless'."

"I think it's wonderful!" his mother said proudly, and went back to bed.

Next day, when his father heard about it, he merely said,

"It seems a roundabout way to make a doorbell

work! I can't see what use it's going to be."

It was to be a long time before Mr Marconi realised just what his son had invented — the very first kind of radio!

Young Marconi was not upset by his father's lack of interest in his wireless. In the spring, when the weather grew warmer, he began to experiment in the large garden round the family house. He fixed large metal plates on poles to his transmitter, and a long length of wire to his receiver (this was what we call an *aerial*). Gradually he managed to make his wireless work over greater and greater distances. First he could ring the bell over the whole length of the garden, and then over several kilometres.

But of course, being able to ring a bell many kilometres away was not much good to anyone, just as Mr Marconi had said! So now Marconi made a change in his receiver. He took out the doorbell and put a second Morse key in its place. Then one of his friends waited by the receiver, several kilometres away, and Marconi tapped out a message on the first Morse key, on his transmitter.

And it worked! The second Morse key on the receiver tapped out the same message! Marconi had succeeded in sending a message in Morse code without wires.

He knew his wireless had great possibilities, and his next task was to sell the invention to a company. Nobody in Italy was interested. Marconi was luckier than most inventors, though. His father gave him money to buy what he needed for his work and his mother had friends in England who could help him sell his invention. He left Italy and went to England to see if he could sell his invention to the Post Office there.

In London he met Sir William Preece who was the Engineer-in-Chief of the General Post Office. Sir William had already done some work himself on a type of wireless, and he was interested. He agreed to let Marconi show him his wireless.

The transmitter was set up on the roof of the Post Office in central London, and Marconi put his receiver on a roof half a kilometre away. Then he sent a message in Morse code from his transmitter on the Post Office roof. To his joy the message came through clearly on the receiver.

Sir William was so impressed that he asked Marconi to show his wireless to the Army and the Navy. This again was a complete success. Sir William now wanted to know if Marconi's wireless waves would travel across the sea, from lighthouses to the mainland.

In May 1897, Marconi went to Lavernock Point on the Bristol Channel. Five kilometres out lay the island of Flatholme with its lighthouse. First Marconi set up his transmitter on the island, then he set up his receiver at Lavernock Point, on a rock about twenty metres high.

But when he tried to receive a Morse signal from the island, his wireless did not seem to work. What could be wrong? Then Marconi had a bright idea. He made the aerial of his receiver longer — when it began to pick up the Morse signal!

Next day several scientists came to see the experiment, but a terrible storm had blown up. They all had to sit in a big wooden packing case on the beach, listening hard to the receiver. To start with, they could hear nothing but the noise of the storm. Then came slight crackling sounds. Then suddenly they all heard it — the Morse signal coming from the island.

"The signals have come across the water through thin air!" shouted Marconi, overjoyed. He had shown that his wireless worked across water as well as across land.

Marconi received many letters of congratulation from scientists. He formed his own company to sell his wirelesses to the world, and he received £15 000 for his invention. When you think that he was still only a young man of twenty-three, you can see how unusual he was. Most inventors do not get paid for their inventions, but Marconi was a very good business man — perhaps that was something he inherited from his father!

His invention saved lives, too. When, two years later, a steamship was stranded on the terrible

Goodwin Sands in the English Channel, it sent out
a distress signal by Morse code on its Marconi
wireless. The lighthouse at South Foreland heard
the signal and sent out its lifeboat, which saved all
the crew of the steamship. Its valuable cargo was
also saved — all because of Marconi's invention.
The wireless quickly became known and used in
ships all over the world.

*   *   *   *   *   *

The biggest challenge of all now awaited Marconi
— to send a Morse signal all the way across the
Atlantic Ocean. He set to work to build a much
larger transmitter at Poldhu, the most south-
westerly point in England.

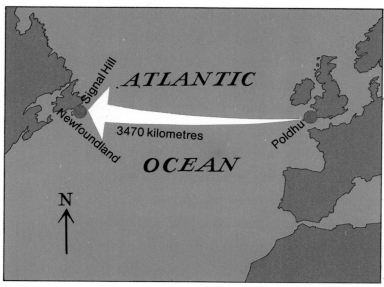

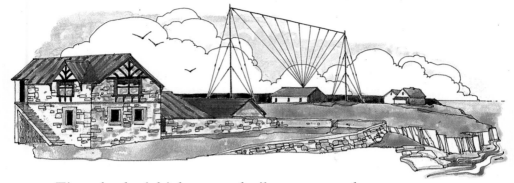

First, he had high masts built, to carry the very long aerial which would be needed to send out signals all the way across the Atlantic. He also built a large petrol engine. This was to drive an electric generator to make the electricity needed for the giant sparks which would send out the Morse signal. The sparks were so big they looked like fireworks!

Then in December of that year, 1901, Marconi went by ship to the rocky coast of Newfoundland, in Canada. There he set up his receiver in an old army camp on top of a hill, which he called Signal Hill. A very long aerial was needed to pick up the signals, so he had balloons made to take his aerial high into the air.

Every day at mid-day, the transmitter at Poldhu was already sending out its Morse signals — the three dots of the letter "S". Marconi was anxious. Were they going to receive the signals, all the way across the Atlantic?

When they sent the first balloon up, with the aerial of copper wire trailing behind, it went up so quickly that it snapped the wire. Then it disappeared into the clouds.

"Balloons are no good!" Marconi told his men. "We'll have to use a kite instead," he added, making up his mind quickly.

The next day, the twelfth of December, was the day of the great test. Marconi was up at six a.m. A strong gale had blown up in the night — not the best of weathers to fly a kite in, but they had to go out and try.

All morning the men tried to get the kite to fly in the gale, the copper aerial hanging down from it, leading to the receiver. In the end they managed it, and the kite flew steadily 120 metres above the ground.

By now the men were soaked to the skin and shivering with cold. They went back into their army hut for a drink of hot chocolate and to warm themselves. It was just 11.30 a.m. They still had half an hour to wait before Poldhu began to send out its signal at mid-day exactly.

Marconi had been working all morning without a bite to eat. He tried to eat some bread, but he was far too excited. Slowly the minutes ticked by until at last the hands of the clock pointed to twelve. Poldhu in Cornwall was about to "go on the air".

But when they listened in the headphones, they could hear nothing but crackling. Again and again they checked the receiver to make sure it was working properly. Still nothing!

By now it was 12.30. Marconi was in despair. His plan to send signals across the Atlantic was not going to work. Everyone would laugh at him for being a fool! He had nearly given up hope. Then suddenly he heard faint noises in the headphones, above the howl of the gale. He listened again, and above the crackling and the storm he could hear . . . yes . . . the sound of three dots. He heard it again. There was no mistake — the letter "S" in Morse code was being signalled all the way from Cornwall. He had done it after all!

And with that great achievement, Marconi became famous all over the world, for soon everybody wanted to use his wireless telegraph, as it was called. The government of his own country, Italy, made him a *marchese* or marquis, and he died rich and famous at the age of sixty-three.

In 1920, radio broadcasting started in America and Britain. Marconi's wireless became the radio we know today, and soon speech and music as well as Morse code were being sent over the air.

Next time you turn on your radio, remember how it all started — with an idea in the mind of a young man, who didn't give up until he had turned his idea into an invention that changed the world.

Sending a Spark Through Air

When Marconi made a spark at one end of his attic room, the spark sent out electric waves all over the room. Marconi's receiver picked up these waves at the other end of the room. And this was the beginning of radio.

You can carry out a very simple test to show how a spark can be "picked up" across your room by your radio.

First you can make and see sparks by pulling a nylon shirt or jumper over your head. You can hear crackling as the cloth rubs over your hair. If you do this in the dark, you can actually see the sparks jump between the cloth and your hair.

But these sparks are not strong enough to send waves across a room. You can make a stronger spark simply by switching the electric light on and off. When you do this, a spark jumps across the metal contacts inside the wall switch. But you must NEVER open up the switch to see inside, as mains electricity is very dangerous.

If you turn a wall switch on and off in the dark, you may be able to see a spark through the space between the lever you press and the plastic casing.

Now for the test. Place a portable radio some way from the wall switch. Turn on the radio but tune it so that it is not on a station — so that it is almost silent. Then turn the switch on and off. You should hear distinct clicks from the radio. There you are! You have sent an electric spark, or the waves from it, across the room from the switch to the radio. This is just like Marconi sending his first spark "message" across his laboratory in his attic.

He Led the Attack on the "King of Diseases"

Ronald Ross never forgot his early childhood days in the vast and beautiful country of India. He was born there, at a place called Almora, in 1857. His father was a soldier, and later became a general, in the Indian Army that helped to rule India when it was a part of the British Empire.

Some of Ronald's memories of his childhood were pleasant. He always remembered riding in a bullock-cart with his mother. The bullocks were big, white, wide-horned cattle.

Another memory was not so pleasant — the look of fear and worry on his mother's face, when his father lay very ill, suffering from malaria.

Luckily Ronald's father did not die, but many people who had malaria did. At that time in India, one million people died from malaria every single year, and it was known as the "king of diseases".

When Ronald was eight, his parents sent him to school in England — a boarding school near Southampton. There he wrote poetry, composed music and painted pictures. His teachers found him a difficult pupil, however, because he was a dreamy, imaginative boy, who always wanted to think things out for himself.

Right up to the time he left school, Ronald had no idea what he wanted to be. So when his father suggested that he should become a doctor, Ronald agreed. In 1874 he became a medical student at St Bartholomew's Hospital in London.

For a long time he was bored by the everyday routine of doctoring, until one day he met a woman who in some way had caught malaria at her home near the Essex marshes.

She complained of feeling cold, then hot, then cold again. She said she suffered from headaches and had pains in her muscles. Ronald was so interested when she described these symptoms that he became excited and frightened the woman away. She never came back, but in the years that followed Ronald was grateful to her. She had given him an interest that was to become his main work in life.

It was very unusual to find a case of malaria in England, because the disease was nearly always found only in hot tropical countries such as India, Africa and South America. People thought it was caused by the smelly air in hot marshy country. Its name comes from the Italian words *male*, meaning "bad" and *aria*, meaning "air".

When Ronald finished his studies and became a

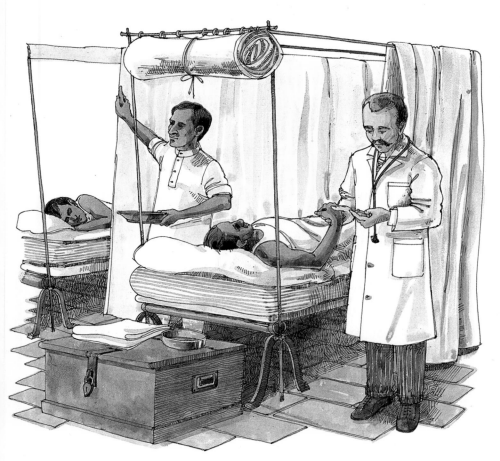

doctor, he joined the Indian Medical Service. He
was sent to Madras, a large town in the south of
India, where he found that most of his work was to
treat soldiers who had malaria. The disease could
be treated by a drug called quinine, but a great
many people died simply from lack of treatment.

Ronald was surprised that the British had done so
little to try to find out what really caused malaria.

85

He did not believe that bad air was the cause. The soldiers who received treatment and lived, were the lucky ones. If the real cause of malaria could be discovered, perhaps something could be done to reduce the appalling death rate amongst the huge population of India.

In 1883, Ronald Ross was given the job of Acting Garrison Surgeon at Bangalore, then one of the more important British bases in India. Like most Europeans in India, he lived in a bungalow.

His bungalow was pleasant, but there were a lot of mosquitoes around it, and this irritated Ronald. He noticed that there seemed to be more mosquitoes around his home than there were in other parts of town, and he wondered why.

Then one day, he saw a swarm of mosquitoes buzzing around a water-tub outside his bedroom window. Looking closely, he saw queer wriggling things in the water. The "wrigglers" were in fact young mosquito grubs, and Ronald realised that mosquitoes were breeding in the water-tub.

He emptied the water away, and after that he found there were not quite so many of the annoying insects around his bungalow. Perhaps, he thought, it might be possible to get rid of mosquitoes altogether, if their breeding places could be filled in,

or drained.

After a year in Bangalore, Ronald began to feel tired and unhappy. He was twenty-seven years old, and he felt that so far, his life had no purpose. He thought of trying to earn his living some other way, perhaps by writing.

He also had a guilty feeling that he ought to be doing more to help the people of India. In particular, he thought he could help to prevent malaria. An idea was gradually forming in his mind that there might be a connection between malaria and mosquitoes.

Dr Manson   Dr Laveran

So Ronald remained a doctor and for the next
few years he relieved the boredom he felt with this
life by writing a number of exciting adventure
stories.   But although his stories became very
popular, he never gave up his special interest in
malaria.

It was not until he spent a long holiday in
England between 1894 and 1895, that Ronald Ross
saw clearly the way in which his life's work should
go.   While on a visit to London, he met Dr
Patrick Manson, a great specialist in tropical
diseases, and told him of his suspicion that
mosquitoes had some connection with malaria.

They talked about the work of a French doctor
called Laveran, who had recently found germs
called Plasmodium in the blood of North Africans
who had malaria.   Dr Manson had some microscope

slides of blood taken from sailors who had come from Africa. When Ronald looked at them, he saw the Plasmodium germs infecting the red blood cells.

The puzzle was: how did malaria germs get from sick people into healthy people? You did not catch malaria simply by being with people who were sick with the disease. It was not infectious in any of the usual ways.

Dr Manson agreed with Ronald that mosquitoes might be the link, and at last Ronald Ross saw very clearly what he most wanted to do. He wanted to find Plasmodium germs inside the bodies of mosquitoes — that would show that there was indeed a link between mosquitoes and malaria!

On his return to India in 1895, Ronald began to study the blood of people with malaria. He found out that, inside human red blood cells, the malaria germs grew very big before splitting to form spores (small seedlike cells), which then burst out to infect other cells. He also found, as Laveran had done, that sometimes the malaria germs grew into both crescent-shaped and round forms that stayed in the patients' blood serum (the watery part of the blood).

Then Ronald proved that healthy people caught malaria when they were injected with blood taken from soldiers who were sick with the disease. This gave rise to more questions. Was it possible for blood injections to happen without the hypodermic syringes which doctors used? Could it happen when mosquitoes bit people?

By now Ronald Ross was so interested in malaria that he wanted to spend all his time studying the disease. You might think that the Army authorities would have been pleased to support Ronald's research, but they did not. Instead, he was ordered to travel all over the country doing the routine work of a doctor. He even had to pay his Indian assistants with his own money, but he did not mind that because malaria research was now more important that anything else in his life.

He kept in touch with Dr Manson, who sent him many helpful hints and ideas for new experiments to try. Both men wondered if malaria was caused by drinking water in which germ-infected mosquitoes had died. Ronald Ross proved that this idea was wrong. He began to feel certain that mosquitoes transmitted malaria by biting people. But how was he to prove it?

One of the difficulties was that there were many different sorts of mosquitoes, and it was possible that only one kind could carry malaria germs.

Then one day one of his Indian assistants, Husein Khan, caught a type of mosquito that Ronald had never seen before. He called it a "dapple-wing", because its wings were covered with little spots, or dapples. He tried to get some dapple-wings to feed by sucking the blood from malaria patients, but only the females would do this. Male mosquitoes of any sort never suck blood.

When the females had fed, Ronald killed them and looked carefully at their bodies under his microscope. He found both the crescent-shaped and the round Plasmodium germs in the dapple-wings' blood. These, as Ronald now knew, grew from the small spores which formed inside human blood cells. Then on the twentieth of August 1897, Ronald Ross made his best discovery so far. Inside the stomach wall of a dapple-wing mosquito, he found a round cell-like object. He realised that it must be a kind of big spore, produced by the coming together of the crescent-shaped and the round Plasmodium germs.

News of the discovery was printed in the *British Medical Journal* for December 18th 1897. Ronald Ross had proved that the germs in the dapple-wing mosquitoes were the same as the germs in the blood

of patients ill with malaria. Now he only needed
to find the connection between dapple-wing
mosquitoes and people with malaria. And the final
question in the malaria story was — how did the
big spores in mosquitoes' stomachs cause malaria in
humans?

He solved the problem on the fourth of July 1898.
After many hours searching for germs in the dead
bodies of infected mosquitoes, he found a cluster of
the small kind of spore inside the salivary gland
which led to the insect's mouth. Now he could
work out just how it happened. The big spore
inside the stomach must break up into smaller

spores that then travelled to the mosquito's salivary glands. When a mosquito bit somebody it injected some saliva (to help to make the blood suitable as food for the insect). The Plasmodium malaria germs were injected along with the saliva!

With all its strange changes of size and shape inside both humans and mosquitoes, what a complicated life-cycle the Plasmodium germ had! No wonder that finding the real cause of malaria had been so difficult and had taken so long.

Ronald Ross sent a telegram to England immediately to tell Dr Manson of his latest — and truly greatest — discovery. The message arrived just in time for Dr Manson to announce the news to an important gathering of doctors in Edinburgh. The doctors actually stood up and cheered! Now they could start to attack the dreaded "king of diseases"!

Ronald Ross left the Indian Medical Service and returned to England, where he did not forget to thank Dr Patrick Manson for his part in the work.

He received one of the greatest honours in the world — the Nobel Prize for Medicine — and later, in 1911, he was knighted and became Sir Ronald Ross.

He devoted the rest of his life to teaching people

all over the world how to get rid of mosquitoes. He showed how to kill them by using chemical powders and by destroying their breeding places. For example, if oil is thinly sprayed on the water where mosquitoes breed, it floats on the surface and prevents the young grubs from getting air.

Ronald Ross died in 1932. Despite all his brilliant work against mosquitoes, he did not succeed in putting an end to malaria. This will only happen when all the malaria-transmitting mosquitoes in the world are destroyed — perhaps an impossible task. Even today, large numbers of people die from malaria, in parts of the world where people are too poor or too ignorant to do something about it. But millions more would die, if the secrets of the "king of diseases" had never been uncovered.

Observing Mosquito Larvae

During late June, go and search for "wrigglers" — the water-dwelling larvae of mosquitoes. Look in still ponds, and tanks of standing water.

When you've found some, keep them alive in pond water, in plastic boxes (do not use tap water).

Put in some water weeds — the wrigglers feed on small creatures living amongst the weed — and keep the boxes in the shade.

Just how *does* a mosquito larva swim? And watch how it breathes — by poking its rear-end breathing tube up through the surface. Can you draw a picture of that?

If you watch really closely, you might be lucky enough to see a larva shedding its skin, when it grows too fat for the old one.

In time, the wrigglers change into pupae which float on the water. Look out for the day when an adult mosquito climbs out of its pupa case.

Later the adults mate and the females lay batches of eggs called *rafts*, on still ponds, and the life-cycle starts once more.

The common gnat–a variety of mosquito

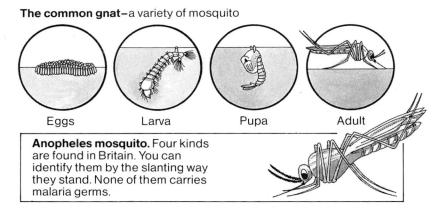

| Eggs | Larva | Pupa | Adult |

Anopheles mosquito. Four kinds are found in Britain. You can identify them by the slanting way they stand. None of them carries malaria germs.

Television's "Dummy" Run

It was just a pile of old junk — a tea chest, a hat box, some darning needles, scrap electric motors and old lenses; a washbowl, a broken radio; some glue, sealing wax and a few other bits and pieces. In 1922, John Logie Baird started to turn that pile of junk into one of the greatest inventions of the twentieth century: the world's first television set.

Early in 1924, he succeeded. It was not a very good set. The black and white picture was very fuzzy and flickery, and it could only be transmitted over a distance of 2.7 metres. Nevertheless, it was the world's very first television picture.

A few days after he managed to produce that first picture, Baird accidentally touched a live electric wire connected to the mains, and was nearly killed. So the world first heard about television through a sensational newspaper story about a penniless inventor who had almost electrocuted himself.

As a result of his dangerous accident, John was asked to leave his attic room in Hastings. He moved to another attic, this time in London, at 22 Frith Street, Soho. While he lived there he met the son of Gordon Selfridge (owner of the famous London department store) and showed him his

incredible machine. John was offered twenty-five pounds a week to display his invention to customers in the store.

His machine was clever, although it was clumsy. It worked by electricity, but it did not use so many electronic parts as do television sets today. The apparatus worked something like this.

A cardboard disc was spun at eighteen turns per second in front of the brightly-lit face of a ventriloquist's dummy. Near the edge of the disc was a ring of holes, arranged in a slight spiral. The spinning holes, one hole at a time, scanned every part of the dummy's face. Each hole scanned one line right across the face.

Disc spins

Photo-electric cell sends strong or weak signals to glow-lamp

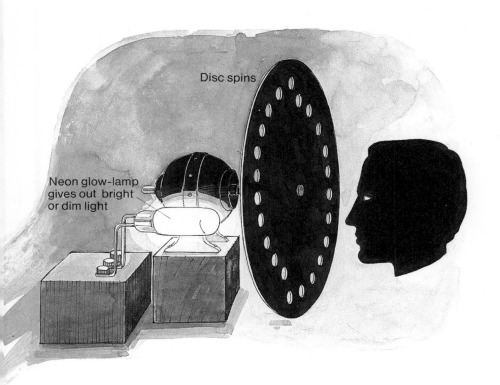

Disc spins

Neon glow-lamp
gives out bright
or dim light

Light reflected off the face passed through the
holes and was focused upon a photo-electric cell.
(*Photo* means "light".) According to whether the
light coming from that part of the face being
scanned was bright or dim, the cell conducted a
strong or a weak electric current. In this way the
picture of the face was broken up into lines (each
line being scanned point by point), and turned into
a code of electric signals.

The code of strong and weak electric signals was

sent to a neon glow-lamp. This lamp was fixed
behind a second disc with holes exactly like those of
the first one — and also spinning at eighteen turns
per second. The strong and weak signals made the
lamp glow brightly or dimly, while the disc with
the holes put back together an image of the face.

People looking through the spinning holes towards
the glow-lamp saw a television picture. Their
brains automatically "put together" the dots and
lines, to make a whole picture in their minds.

Customers thronged into Selfridges, curious to
see the picture of a ventriloquist's dummy
"magically" transmitted from one place to another.

An article devoted to the invention appeared in
Nature, the important scientific magazine.

Then in January 1926, John Logie Baird
demonstrated his improved apparatus to learned
members of the Royal Institution. Everybody was
impressed — except for one old gentleman whose
beard became entangled in the machinery!

During the following year, 1927, Baird ran the
world's first television station — 2 TV — in
London. (The first radio station's call sign was
2LO.) The signals were carried on radio waves,
and they were transmitted from London to Harrow,
a distance of nineteen kilometres.

The year after, Baird transmitted the cheerful wooden face of "Bill" the dummy from London to New York — and to an ocean liner in mid-Atlantic. The poor inventor from a Hastings attic was now a famous man. John Logie Baird was no longer poor, but he never became a rich man, in spite of his wonderful invention.

At first the British Broadcasting Corporation refused to have anything to do with television. Then in 1929, it was forced by an Act of Parliament to start making experimental television transmissions, using the Baird system. Baird improved the apparatus to give brighter if not sharper pictures, but the BBC stopped using the Baird system in 1937, when modern television broadcasting started.

Our modern system is a method which depends upon beams of electrical particles called electrons. The picture, however, is scanned in lines with light and dark patches in much the same way as in the world's very first television picture, all those years ago.

"Dotty" Pictures on TV

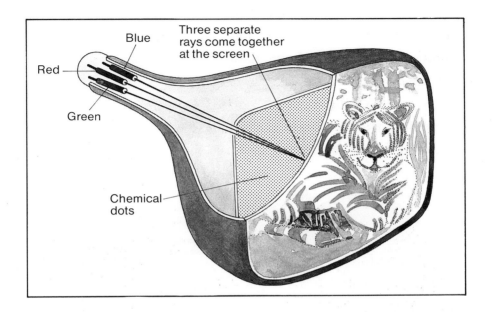

Inside a colour TV set, three rays keep sweeping across the back of the screen. This is called scanning. Each ray stands for a colour: red, green or blue. The colour appears when a ray hits its own special dots of chemical. There are three sorts of chemical dot, one sort for each colour.

When a ray is strong the colour it makes is bright. When a ray is weak the colour it makes is dim. Any colour can be made from a mixture of red, green and blue.

Every time a ray scans the screen its dots shine bright or dim. The pictures we see are really lines of red, green and blue dots. The dots make twenty-five pictures per second. Each picture shows a little more of the action than the one before it.

In a wonderful way that nobody fully understands, your brain makes sense of the "dotty" pictures, to make moving pictures.

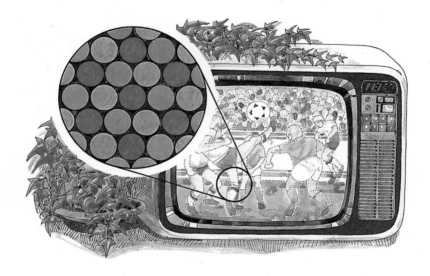

Can Chimps Talk?

Can chimpanzees talk? That sounds like a silly
question — but is it? Chimps whoop, grunt and
whistle to each other across the forest but they
cannot make the same kind of sounds as humans do.
Nor can chimps understand the sounds we make.
But it is possible to talk without sounds. People
who are very deaf or who cannot speak can learn
another language which does not use sounds. They
can learn a special sign language for the deaf and
dumb: they use their hands and fingers to make
sign words. It is not difficult to learn and twenty
years or so ago scientists thought of trying to teach

it to chimps. Chimps could not talk but they might
be able to learn the deaf-and-dumb sign language.

The first people to teach a sign language to
chimps were two American scientists, Beatrice and
Allen Gardner. They began in 1965 with a female
chimp called Washoe who lived in a caravan behind
the Gardner's ranch house near the Rocky
Mountains.

First the Gardners taught Washoe the sign for
"hat". They showed Washoe a real hat and then
showed her the sign for "hat". This sign is made
by placing your hand on your head, so the Gardners
placed Washoe's hand on her head. Then they
taught her the sign for "flower". Again they
showed her a real flower and then made her touch
her nose with her fingertips. Each time Washoe
made the correct sign the Gardners gave her a
raisin as a reward. Washoe seemed to like the
game of sign making, and besides, she got it right
all the time. Too many raisins and she might
get fat! She also liked looking at magazines,
particularly the ones with coloured pictures. She
would point at a picture in a magazine and, in sign
language, ask "What's that?"

By the age of four Washoe had learnt about
eighty-five signs. Then she had a son, Lulas,

Hat

Flower

and she taught him some of the signs she knew.
It seemed that Washoe really had learnt sign
language.

By now the Gardners were fascinated by the
chimps. They wanted to do more experiments on
teaching very young chimps so they brought three
new "pupils" to their school. Three four-day old
chimps, called Moja, Tatu and Dar, came to the
ranch. These names are numbers in the African
language of Swahili: moja means "one" in
Swahili, tatu means "three" and dar means "four".
There had been another chimp called Pili, which
means "two" in Swahili, but she died very young.
Of the three chimps Moja and Tatu were female
and Dar was male.

Each chimp was given special rooms to live and
sleep in. Each had a bedroom, a playroom, a
bathroom and a kitchen-dining room. There were
three human helpers for each chimp and all the
helpers spoke the sign language. It was forbidden
to speak English in front of the chimps. The
helpers had to use sign language all the time they
were with the chimps. There was a good reason
for this.

Children learn to talk by hearing their parents
and other adults speak. They learn that certain

sounds make up certain words and that different words mean different things. If there were different words for the same thing then it would be much more difficult to learn to talk. That is why the helpers only used sign language with the chimps. They did not want to muddle them by speaking English as well as using sign language.

Part of the helpers' job was to make sure that the chimps lived as much like human children as possible. They were learning to use human language and it was important that they lived as much like humans as possible. The chimps' day began at seven o'clock in the morning when the helpers woke them up and sent them off to wash and clean themselves. Next came breakfast — fruit and a glass of warm milk. The chimps were

messy eaters and so they had to wear bibs — just
like human babies.

After breakfast the chimps dressed themselves in
shirt and jeans. Unless it was very hot they had
to wear clothes. Next they helped make their beds
and tidy their rooms. They even helped with the
washing-up after breakfast. Every morning the
chimps went to "school". They had a half-hour
lesson in sign language; learning new signs and
practising old ones. Half an hour was about the
right length of time — after that the chimps

became bored. They had playtime and then another half-hour lesson. The second lesson was a practical one; they looked at books or magazines, painted, scribbled on note pads and sorted wooden blocks. Before lunch they had a short nap.

Lunch was fruit and milk again, and there were more lessons in the afternoon. They did some painting in the afternoon as well, so by 6.30 the chimps were ready for their bath. They loved that. They sploshed and splashed and everybody got very wet. It took a long time to get dry, especially since it was important that the chimps had dry hair. If they went to bed with wet hair they might catch a cold, so there was always an hour's playtime before bed at 7.45.

The chimps were very different, just as human beings are. Moja was the quiet one. She was rather afraid of things like the metal trays for making ice in the fridge. Tatu liked dressing up and sewing and she was very interested in the colours she wore. Dar liked toys, especially his toy cow and his cuddly blanket.

Moja liked to carry Tatu on her back and learnt to use the sign for "there". She would point to her back, make the sign for "there", and Tatu would climb on her back. She also called Dar

110

"baby" in sign language and she liked to cuddle him and feed him from his bottle.

This work with the chimps has shown that they can learn the deaf-and-dumb sign language and they can use it to talk to each other. Moja knew about 150 words and Tatu more than sixty. They could say to each other "come play" or "come tickle". They could make up whole sentences about things, such as "a cork is different from a key". Perhaps this does not sound very exciting but it does show that their minds work in the same way as those of small human children.

The difference between humans and chimps is that as human children grow older they learn more and more words and more and more ideas. We all go on learning through all our lives. So far, it seems that the chimps can learn only so much sign language. They cannot keep on getting better at using it. The Gardners' work is still going on, though.

The First Astronauts

The conquest of space must be counted as one of
the greatest of human achievements, even in a
century full of such achievements. The honour of
being the first human being in space goes to the
Russian, Yuri Gagarin. On the twelfth of April
1961 he circled the earth in the spacecraft *Vostok* at
a speed of over 27 000 kilometres an hour. His
journey took just one hour forty-eight minutes!

Then, less than a month later, on the fifth of May
1961, Commander Alan Shepard became the first
American in space, in the spacecraft *Freedom 7*.

The whole world admired the bravery of the astronauts, but how many people really knew how much sheer hard work went into the preparation for such flights as these?

The word *astronaut* means "sailor of the stars". The American astronauts were the first spacemen whose adventures were filmed for everybody to see. They told people what their training was like, and how it felt to be "star sailors", at a time when there were few facts known about living in space; there were only theories.

Spacemen need to be daring and brave; they also need to keep calm and act carefully if they are in trouble. Since spacecraft are similar to very complicated aircraft, it is not surprising that the first people selected to be trained as astronauts were all pilots of jet fighter planes. Several of them had won medals for bravery in wartime. They were men who had already proved that they could, in times of danger, still operate complex instrument panels within the small cramped area of a fighter plane cockpit.

All the jet pilots who wanted to be astronauts were tested in the Aero Medical Laboratory of the Air Development Center at Dayton, Ohio. Doctors tested the pilots' heart, blood, eyesight and intelligence. The doctors also wanted to make sure that the men had fast reflexes and reaction times. (*Reaction time* measures how long it takes a man to act after sensing danger. Being a spaceman was certainly going to be dangerous!

Over five hundred jet pilots were at first thought to be suitable to test the new machines that were costing so many millions of pounds to build. Finally, however, only seven men were found to have all the qualities that were needed.

They were Scott Carpenter, Gordon Cooper, John Glenn, Virgil Grissom, Walter Schirra, Donald Slayton and — of course — Alan Shepard.

Scott Carpenter John Glenn Walter Schirra Donald Slayton
Gordon Cooper Virgil Grissom Alan Shepard

In 1959, being an astronaut meant being an engineer, a scientist and a space explorer, all rolled into one. It also meant being a "human guinea-pig" to test the new spacecraft for any possible faults.

Astronauts had to be tough mentally and physically, as well as intelligent, quick and healthy. Their bodies had to withstand enormous G forces (usually called Gs — 1G represents the force of gravity acting on a person on the earth).

To break through the earth's atmosphere into space itself, spacecraft must achieve very great speeds. It is while the spacecraft is accelerating to these speeds that G forces affect the astronauts. As the Gs are increased, the astronaut feels much heavier.

To discover how many Gs they could tolerate, each man rode in a box-like cabin on the outer end of a huge steel arm which was spun sideways, very fast, in a wide circle. The astronauts nicknamed this machine "The Wheel".

As The Wheel spun faster, the number of G forces increased on the man in the cabin. At 6Gs his arms felt six times heavier than normal, and his blood seemed like lead. Alan and his six fellow astronauts used to boast about the number of Gs

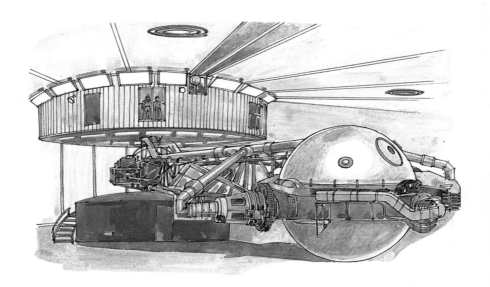

they could tolerate before the machine had to be
stopped. Training machines like The Wheel
helped the astronauts to get the feel of what
blasting off into space might be like.

Another training aid was a thick-walled,
windowless room called an Anechoic Chamber. Its
walls were lined with wedges made of fibreglass
which absorbed every single sound. The astronauts
were trained inside the Anechoic Chamber in pitch
darkness, to prepare them for being utterly alone in
the black silence of outer space.

It was so quiet in the room that people could
even hear their own hearts beating. They couldn't
tell whether it was day or night. The only

furniture was a chair, a table, a bed, a chemical lavatory like those used in a caravan, and a refrigerator filled with sandwiches and drinks. Wires fixed to the astronauts' ankles led to instruments outside the room. Doctors could tell, by watching these instruments, if a man was showing any signs of fear, such as sweating, or breathing hard. During the long, dark, silent hours, the astronauts sometimes thought they saw patches of colour and other strange visions, like waking dreams. Many people found the room so horrible that they soon came out.

Another unpleasant training machine was the "Hot Box". There is almost no air in space, and the earth's atmosphere is almost solid by comparison. The scientists were sure that when the spacecraft returned to earth at a speed of thousands of kilometres an hour, it would hit the air in our atmosphere and rub against it so hard that the outer covering of the spacecraft would get red hot and start to burn. This is called *friction*. When meteors meet the frictional forces of the air around the earth, they glow with heat, and we call them *shooting stars*. So the "Hot Box" was to help the astronauts to get used to working normally in a very high temperature.

As well as suffering the tortures of the training machines, the astronauts had to help to improve the design of the spacecraft. There was so much to learn about sending people into space that all seven men decided to specialise, then work as a team. Each man learnt all there was to know about a subject, then reported only the most important ideas to his fellows.

Scott Carpenter specialised in knowing about how the scientists and engineers on the ground would communicate with the spacemen by radio.

Alan Shepard was the specialist in how the height, flight and speed of the spacecraft would be followed by tracking stations on land, and on ships, around the world. Alan was also responsible for understanding how a spacecraft would be found when it was parachuted into the sea, and how an astronaut would be rescued by helicopter.

Walter Schirra worked on improving the spacesuits and helmets which the men would need to wear. To find out how a spacesuit could stand up to heat, he spent ten minutes at the sizzling temperature of 180°F (62°C) inside a heat chamber. The important thing was that the oxygen supply to the suit had to work properly at great heat. There was no need for the other astronauts to try the test.

Walter reported all they needed to know.

Gordon Cooper and Donald Slayton studied the powerful rocket engines that would boost the spacecraft at lift-off time. Virgil Grissom helped to design the final layout of the spacecraft's controls.

Although the astronauts were all very different as people, they trusted each other and rarely had arguments. They felt responsible for each other. It helped them to know, too, that their wives and children were also firm friends.

*   *   *   *   *   *

Alan Shepard did not expect to be chosen as the first American to ride into space. Although the other six astronauts were quick to congratulate him, Alan knew that they must be feeling disappointed.

America's first spacecraft were of the Mercury type, named after Mercury, the swift messenger of the Greek gods. Alan's Mercury spacecraft was called *Freedom 7*.

Once chosen, Alan spent many hours of the next few weeks checking over the Redstone booster rocket, with its bell-shaped Mercury spacecraft mounted on top. He practised getting ready for the flight forty times! Doctors kept checking to see that he was keeping fit. They even wanted to know how nervous Alan felt, as the day for launching *Freedom 7* drew near.

At first the launch date was fixed for the second of May 1961. The place was Cape Canaveral, Florida, close to the sea.

Early that morning, when Alan looked out of his window, he could see the giant rocket waiting on its concrete launching pad, lit up by a bright searchlight. Preparations for the launching had already begun, but heavy rain was falling and lightning flashed in the sky.

Alan dressed in his spacesuit and was taken by lift to the top of the tower which stood next to the rocket on the launch pad. Just as he was about to cross a narrow bridge to get on board his spacecraft, he was told that the flight was being cancelled. The weather was too bad.

The flight finally took place on the fifth of May. On that great day, Alan Shepard crossed the little bridge leading to *Freedom 7*, wearing his bulky spacesuit. He squeezed into the tiny spacecraft — *Freedom 7* was only about the size of a telephone box! All round him there were meters, switches, buttons, levers, dials and coloured lights. Alan lay down on a couch made of metal-walled, bubble-like

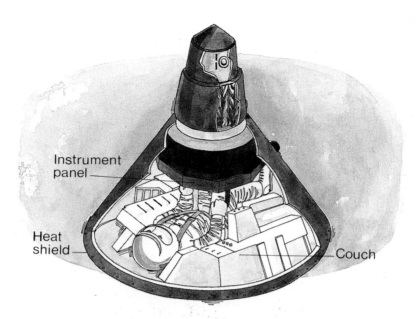

Instrument panel

Heat shield

Couch

spaces, and lined with foam rubber.   Then he
strapped himself in.

Outside, and far below, the final checking time of
the countdown had begun.   There were last-minute
delays while engineers made their final safety checks.
Alan had to lie there waiting for about four hours!
He started to get a little worried, and his heart beat
faster, but he was glad to know that there was an
"escape tower" mounted on top of his craft.

The escape tower held small rockets and
parachutes.   If there was any danger of the
Redstone rocket blowing up, the escape tower would
shoot the spacecraft out of danger and parachute it
safely down to the ground.

At last all systems were "Go", which meant that everything had been checked one last time, and worked properly. Lift-off was at 09.34 hours in the morning. The rocket engines fired with a roar like thunder, but Alan kept calm inside his cabin. The G forces increased as the rocket accelerated, making his body feel like lead. At one time during his flight he felt a force of 11Gs! The rumble of the rocket, however, was quieter than he had expected.

Alan Shepard's flight into space lasted only fifteen minutes. He did not go into orbit. The shape of his flight path up and down was like that of a bullet fired up into the sky, only to fall back again. The booster rocket reached a speed of 8000 kilometres an hour, before it sent *Freedom 7* flying at a height of 185 kilometres. Then the huge rocket fell into the sea, its purpose over. It was just then that Alan Shepard lived through a few moments in which he felt that he had no weight at all.

During the short flight, Alan tested the small control rocket motors which could make the spacecraft move up, down or sideways. He also tested the retro rockets which acted as brakes when *Freedom 7* dropped back into the atmosphere. The heat-proof spacesuit worked too — Alan kept cool even when friction made the spacecraft glow red hot on its downward trip.

Freedom 7 landed by parachute in the sea, 480 kilometres from where it had been launched only fifteen minutes earlier. There Alan Shepard was rescued by helicopter, to become America's Number One Spaceman. It was to be another year before John Glenn became the first American astronaut to go into orbit round the earth.

Are You Quick on the Draw?

Put a penny on the back of your hand. Twist your hand over, to make the penny fall. Then try to catch the penny before it reaches the ground. Try this test ten times. How many catches did you score?

The time you take to catch the penny after it starts to fall is your *reaction time*. Some people have very fast reaction times — astronauts, pilots of jet planes and racing car drivers. Because of the speeds at which they travel, they must act instantly at the slightest hint of danger. But quick reaction times are nothing new — cowboys in the days of the pioneering West had to be quick on the draw — to stay alive!

Try that penny again — and again. Are you getting better with practice? Try your left hand — is it slower than your right hand?

When you've practised for a while, try it on your friends. Are their reaction times as good as yours?

Index